Your Day In Court

Your Day In Court

Navigating Your Way Through The Courts

Russell B. Franzen

Writers Club Press
San Jose New York Lincoln Shanghai

Your Day In Court
Navigating Your Way Through The Courts

Writers Club Press
an imprint of iUniverse.com, Inc.

For information address:
iUniverse.com, Inc.
5220 S 16th, Ste. 200
Lincoln, NE 68512
www.iuniverse.com

ISBN: 0-595-16131-6

Printed in the United States of America

For Emily:
Drive Safe, Drive Sober, Drive Smart

Salus populi suprema est lex
The good of the people is the chief law

Cicero

Contents

Foreword xiii

Chapter 1
Traffic Court—A Rigged Deck? 3

    How Is The Deck Stacked? 4

    Who's Who? 6

Chapter 2
Common Misconceptions That Cost You Money 8

    License Plates 8

    No Proof of Insurance 9

    Speeding 10

    "Michigan Stops Are Okay." 11

    Seat Belts 12

    Tinted Windows 12

    Dangle-y Things 13

Chapter 3
What Do I Do With This Ticket? 14

The Ticket—Your Special Invitation *14*

Civil Infractions *15*

Check the Ticket *16*

Material Defects *16*

PIN defects *17*

Decisions, Decisions *18*

Your Options *19*

A Word About Defaults *22*

So you want to have a Hearing *23*

Questions To Ask The Clerk *27*

Chapter 4
Your Hearing   31

Preparing Your Defense *31*

Get to the Point *37*

Perspective, perspective, perspective *37*

Rehearse *38*

Adjournments *38*

On the Day of the Hearing *39*

The Hearing *41*

Common Courtroom Mistakes *43*

Sanctions *44*

A Word About Points *46*

Waiving Fines and Costs *48*

After The Hearing-More Waiting *49*

Appeals *49*

Formal Hearing *50*

Chapter 5
Misdemeanors 52

Probable Cause *53*

Arraignment *53*

A Word About Court Appointed Attorneys... .... *54*

If The Court Accepts The Guilty Plea *58*

Be Prepared To Pay *60*

Pre-Sentence Investigations *61*

Probation *62*

Not Guilty Plea *64*

Chapter 6
Small Claims   66

Filing The Case *67*

Preparing Your Small Claims Case *69*

Settling The Case *72*

Appeals *72*

Collecting The Judgment *73*

Chapter 7
The Courthouse Wedding 75
Afterword 79
About the Author 83
Appendix 1   Traffic Accident? 85
Appendix 2   Thank You, Zolton! 87
Appendix 3   Web Sites Of Interest 89

Foreword

During the time I spent in the court system, many lawyers and police offi-cers came to me with questions. "How does the court work?" "What does the judge look for in my testimony?" "What happens if I am late for court?"

They knew I did not have a law degree. Instead, I had something the law schools and police academies do not teach: knowledge of the court system.

Although the principles in this book apply to most courts, this book concentrates on the Michigan District Courts. They are the busiest of Michigan's courts and the part of the court system where all criminal cases begin. They are the home of the traffic and small claims courts, and civil cases where damages are less than $25,000.00.

Chances are, if you ever have to go to court, you will go to the district court.

To all the hundreds of people who told me that the whole court process is a "money game," I am now able to give you the entire answer. When I worked in the system my answer was "No, it is not. Since you cannot go to jail for speeding, the only alternative is a prohibitive fine." This was, in theory, correct.

Now, I add to my answer that "Yes, it is a 'money game.'" Municipalities make no apologies for increasing their volume of tickets because the lion's share of the money collected from a ticket written under their local ordinance goes into that community's general fund. One community I am aware of bases their entire police budget on ticket revenue. They are probably not alone.

What began as something honorable is now often "a stacked deck."

It is, therefore, difficult for you and I to win this "money game." By knowing what the playing field is like, however, you increase your chances.

I want to make this book as simple as possible. This is not a law book. It is not written for people familiar with the courts. It is more of a road map that hits the major highways and thoroughfares. To get around on side streets, you will have to ask for further directions. The service stations that give those kind of directions have signs on them saying "Law Office."

I will only try to hit what I think are the high points, the ones most people need to be familiar with. The volume of new laws and court rules going into effect during each legislative session are staggering, meaning that if I get into too much detail, the book may be outdated by the time it gets into print.

Until the legislature has the guts to reform the auto insurance laws, you and I have to rely on the good judgment and discretion of police officers, magistrates and judges to keep inequity at bay.

Hopefully, this book will help you navigate those rough waters.

Your Day In Court

Chapter 1

Traffic Court—A Rigged Deck?

A friend of mine in the legal business once described traffic court as a "rigged deck." He was correct in the sense that the deck is stacked against the person who gets a ticket. Nevertheless, I continue to believe that any time you feel you were wrongly ticketed, you should have your day in court.

"But," you say, "I am a good driver. I will not have to go to court." The truth is, with so many laws on the books, even the most pious among us break a law every now and then. Don't believe me?

Did you ever let a parking meter expire while your car remained parked? Did your speed ever creep over 1 mph over the posted speed limit? Did you ever drive with a tail light out (whether you knew it was out or not)?

Gotcha!

OK, so you did not swipe something or cause damage to property. Nevertheless, you broke the law. We all do. And at some point, all of us will get a special invitation to appear in court.

A quick word about the title of this chapter: Michigan has no "traffic court." Traffic cases are heard in the District Court as either misdemeanor or

3

civil infraction cases. A majority of District Court cases involve traffic so, to keep things simple, I will refer to the place where traffic civil infractions are heard as "traffic court."

How Is The Deck Stacked?

In 1979, the legislature decriminalized most moving traffic violations. This meant that if you received a speeding ticket, you could no longer request a jury trial. On the other hand, you could not go to jail if found responsible.

They called this new category of offenses "civil infractions," meaning that you broke the law, but your action was not serious enough that you would have to go to jail for it.

Considering that, usually, more than half of the cases in the district court are civil infractions, it was probably a good move. Court dockets and jails would, otherwise, be irreparably logjammed.

The move toward civil infractions, however, created something of a monster. It put the courts in the business of making money.

Most of the courts in Michigan turn a profit, meaning that there is money left over after the court's budget is satisfied. Here is a thumbnail sketch of how the court's funding system works.

When the jurist assesses "court costs," that money goes into the general fund of the unit of government charged by law with running that court. That unit of government is the court's "funding unit."

Usually, the funding unit is a county. Some individual communities (most are in Wayne and Kent Counties) or groups of cities and townships are funding units, too. The funding unit approves the court's budget and provides it with money to meet that budget.

After the court's budgetary needs are satisfied, the funding unit has money left over that it can use for anything it wishes. This is, of course, money that is not raised through taxing the general population, which is a dream come true for the local politicians.

As a taxpayer, this can be good news, since tax rates are not raised as often. As a driver, this is bad news, because the community gets used to the extra money generated by the court costs, resulting in police officers writing more tickets.

In communities where the fine money goes to libraries, as the law requires, the libraries flourish (see Monroe). If a new courthouse is built, chances are good that the money is coming from ticket revenue, either as a direct fee or from the collected court costs. I already mentioned the police department I know of that gets its entire police department budget from ticket revenue.

Despite what you just read, I am not implying that police officers are writing dubious tickets to enrich someone's coffers. I do not believe that. I *do* believe that departments are being more aggressive in their enforcement because of the monetary incentive to their communities. Bigger budgets mean bigger raises.

Try this sometime: Find a parking lot near a major intersection and park where you have a clear view of one of the traffic lights and the intersection. For added realism, have some coffee in a cardboard cup and a powdered donut (just kidding!).

If you can go ten minutes without seeing a vehicle in the intersection while that vehicle's light is red ("But officer, when I looked, the light was yellow!") or someone coast through a right-turn-on-red ("But that is a Michigan Stop. Everybody knows it is okay to do that."), I will be very surprised.

My point is that there are so many laws on the books that it is impossible not to break one. The best we can hope for is to not be obvious about it. Because it is so easy to find "lawbreakers," police officers do not need to make up an offense against a driver or write a ticket for a marginal offense. Aggressive enforcement is simply writing tickets for offenses that, at another time, either did not exist or might have been ignored.

Who's Who?

In Michigan, each District Court Judge handles thousands of cases each year. To help them out, the legislature allows the chief judge to appoint a magistrate.

The District Court Magistrate is, in effect, an unelected judge who sits at the pleasure of the court's judges. The magistrate must be a registered voter in the court district he/she serves in and the appointment must meet with the approval of the funding unit. The limits of a magistrate's authority are set by law, with the chief district court judge deciding how much ultimate authority he/she has within those boundaries.

The magistrate need not be an attorney, although only magistrates who are attorneys are allowed to hear small claims cases.

Lest you think that a non-attorney magistrate is inferior to an attorney-magistrate (the designations are mine. The law makes no such distinctions), I must say that most of the best magistrates I met while in the court system were not attorneys.

The chief district judge outlines the magistrate's authority in a local administrative order that is filed with the State Court Administrative Office (SCAO), which is the administrative arm of the Michigan Supreme Court.

The district judge can, without a hearing, overrule a magistrate's decision. This is a rare practice, but its availability underscores the oversight responsibility of judges over magistrates.

Because the duties of the district court judges and magistrates are largely the same for the court functions covered in this book, I will use the inclusive term "jurist" where applicable.

Chapter 2

Common Misconceptions That Cost You Money

License Plates

"I can have until the end of the month to renew my registration."

"If I get a ticket for Expired Plates, I can take in proof that I got new ones and the court will dismiss the ticket."

Wrong, and Wrong Again. The law requires that a driver provide a police officer a valid driver license, proof of insurance, and registration upon demand. If your registration is not valid, neither is your license plate. You may even get a ticket for Expired Plates or Improper Plates to go along with your registration violation.

If your plate is valid and you left the registration paperwork at home, you may get a ticket for No Proof of Registration (you could not prove the vehicle is registered even though the officer has called in the plate number and knows the plate status and that it is registered to you, the person whose driver license he holds in his hand.) This is a ticket where the fine and costs will be waived if you show proof at the court before the appearance date. Some courts actually dismiss these tickets, although the law only requires that they waive the fine and costs. The difference is that if fine and costs are waived, the offense still shows up on your driving record. If dismissed, it does not show up on the record.

No Proof of Insurance

This is another case where you may think the ticket will be dismissed if you show your proof to the court before your appearance date. Not so.

The law *permits* a fine of $10, but *requires* the courts to collect a $25 fee on each No Proof of Insurance violation, even if proof is later shown. Some courts still dismiss these tickets if proof is shown, but they are becoming harder to find. The $25 fee, which goes to the funding unit, is difficult for the communities to give away.

While the fine cannot exceed $10, costs can go as high as $100 on these violations. Add the $24 mandatory state fees and you could get charged $159 even though you had insurance in effect at the time of the traffic stop.

One seldom used provision of the law allows the court to take the driver license of a person determined to be responsible for a No Proof of Insurance violation if the person does not have insurance on the vehicle on the court date.

Speeding

"If you go with the flow of traffic, you will not be stopped."

Does the phrase "shooting fish in a barrel" mean anything to you? If your group is speeding and the traffic enforcement device of choice is the laser speed measurement device, the phrase is literally true. A trained officer could easily pick off every car in the group.

If the officer is using a radar and the group shoots back a speed over the limit, the officer could pull you over (or anyone else in the group, for that matter) and probably make the charge stick.

"They will not pull me over if I am only going 3 miles an hour over the limit."

This may be true. Just remember that any time you travel over the speed limit, you gamble. The law does not say you can have three miles an hour over the limit. Or five. Or seven. Individual departments and officers set those limits. The speed limit is the highest speed you can travel at without getting a ticket.

The reason officers grant some leeway is because they realize the driver's speedometer can be wrong. A speedometer is a moving part on your car. All other moving parts wear out over time. So, the older the car and the more miles on it, you can pretty well bet that there is a difference between the true speed and the one listed on your speedometer. Other factors, such as tire size and transmission wear, can also give you a wrong speed reading.

Let us imagine that Officer Jones is running a radar unit and is allowing drivers three miles an hour over the posted limit before he pulls them over. You are driving at what your speedometer says is 3 miles an hour over the limit, but your car has 120,000 miles on it and, although your speedometer says you are going 73 mph, you are actually traveling at 76 mph.

And the excuse that "I had my cruise control set at 73" simply tells the police officer or jurist that you were intentionally driving over the limit. Intent to speed is not an element of the offense, but the jurist will still take note of the admission.

"Michigan Stops Are Okay."

A "Michigan Stop" is one of the many names given to a rolling stop. The Michigan Vehicle Code defines "stop" as a "complete cessation of movement." Anything less can buy you a ticket.

It is common for us to apply pressure to the brake until we feel a little jolt, then proceed. It may feel like we stopped, but the forward momentum never really ceases.

I recommend a two-second rule. It takes about two seconds after the stop to look both ways, leaving no doubts in the officer's mind that you stopped.

Seat Belts

"I was wearing my seat belt! I had the strap under my arm because it is more comfortable. I should not have this ticket!"

The law does not require the seat belt to be comfortable. It does say, however, that the belt must be properly adjusted and fastened. The belts were designed to be worn over the shoulder. If the officer sees it being worn any other way (or with too much slack in it) you will get a ticket.

Tinted Windows

"I only had a 30% tint on my windshield. Why did I get a ticket?"

The law says, and I am paraphrasing here, that on the windshield and front side windows, only four inches of tint is allowed along the top to cut down on glare. Tinting is allowed on the back and side windows.

If the driver's eyes are sensitive to light, an eye doctor can "prescribe" window tinting. That "prescription" should be kept with the driver's registration and proof of insurance so that a tinted window ticket is not issued.

Dangle-y Things

"It is so cool to have this fragrant pine tree hanging from my rearview mirror!"
Cool is in the eyes of the beholder. If a police officer wants to pull you over, sees it, and has no other reason, you will be pulled over for the offense of "Obstructed Vision." The offense is serious enough to have two points attached to it.

The law prohibits a person from driving with a "dangling ornament or other suspended object…which obstructs the vision of the driver of the vehicle."

It is unlikely that an officer will pull someone over for a "dangling ornament," but the law is broad enough to give them that authority.

Chapter 3

What Do I Do With This Ticket?

The Ticket—Your Special Invitation

You are driving along, minding your own business, when you see a police car parked up ahead, facing in your direction. Instinctively, your foot leaves its resting place on the accelerator. You look down to a speedometer that says 73 miles an hour. You let it drop to 70 and continue at that pace. You pass the police car, which pulls out in your direction. One mile later, the red bubble light is flashing right behind you. You were not speeding, you explain to the officer.

You get a ticket anyway. For driving at 75 in a 70 m.p.h. zone.

Civil Infractions

The ticket you receive alleges that you committed a type of "crime" known as a civil infraction. It is not really a crime, though. A civil infraction means that you broke a law but the infraction is not serious enough for a person to go to jail for doing it.

For sanctions, civil infractions have civil fines, court costs and fees and, sometimes, community service. A person cannot go to jail for committing a civil infraction.

In return for dropping the criminal penalties for these offenses in 1979, jury trials with their accompanying legal rights are not allowed and a person can be found "responsible" by a preponderance (51%) of the evidence, as opposed to proof beyond a reasonable doubt.

Some traffic cases are misdemeanors. For those, a person can go to jail (although it is unlikely unless that person is a serious scoff law) and have a jury trial, if desired. We will discuss those in the chapter devoted to misdemeanors.

Now that you have the ticket in hand, you may wonder what all of that information means. All of it is important to the court, the police, and/or the secretary of state.

Check the Ticket

The first thing to do when you get home is check the ticket for accuracy. There are certain things the law requires must be written on a ticket. There are some things that can get you in trouble if they are missing or incorrect.

Material Defects

If something required by law is not present, the ticket has a material defect. Think about it. If you receive a ticket, but your name, date of birth, or driver license number is missing, how can you be identified?

It is possible, though not certain, that a jurist will dismiss the ticket if these are not present. It is more likely that the jurist will allow the officer to amend the ticket at the hearing.

In a traffic civil infraction, it is alleged that a section of the motor vehicle code was violated by the person named on the ticket. A risky strategy at an informal hearing might be one like this:

Defendant: Your Honor, this ticket is no good. There is no name on the ticket, so I ask the court to dismiss it.

Jurist: How did you come into possession of this ticket?

Defendant: uh…

Jurist: Officer Jones, who did you give this ticket to?

Officer: To the person whose driver license number is on the ticket. I recognize this person standing next to me as the one I gave the ticket to.

Jurist: Motion denied.

Another material defect is an unsigned ticket. The Michigan State Police and a few local police departments do not sign the original tickets until they return to their department and review the tickets for accuracy. This means that the defendant's copy is not signed and could be different than the original. This practice is tolerated because only the lack of information on the original ticket makes it defective.

PIN defects

Most defects found on tickets are just a pain in the neck (PIN), because they cause extra work for court clerks, police officers and defendants. Some common PIN defects are:

Incorrect address. If the address on the ticket is wrong, your notices from the court may not be delivered, or they may arrive late. If the address is wrong because you moved and did not change your address with the secretary of state, you are lucky the officer did not write you up for that, too. In any event, call the court and give them your correct address.

Color of the car. I cringe when I think of how many people pin their hopes of winning their case on the fact that the officer, at 2:30 AM, mistook their forest green car for dark blue.

Decisions, Decisions

So the officer gave you a ticket and told you to have a nice day (can't they find something less offensive to say after they just ruined your day?). You drop the ticket on the seat next to you and resume your journey.

Do not lose that ticket!

Depending on the court, you have between ten and thirty days to tell the court how you want to proceed. This is known as "appearing" in court. (Your appearance date is located near the bottom of the ticket). The normal time period is about 14 days, but the law leaves the appearance date to the discretion of the court and/or officer.

Most courts allow you to "appear" and set a court date by telephone. Some, however, do not. Contact the court as soon as possible to find out. Again, the normal time limit is about fourteen days, but it varies from court to court. Make sure you know when your deadline is.

The court's telephone number is located near the bottom of the traffic ticket. If you are fortunate, the police officer will, along with the ticket, hand you a ticket-sized information sheet. These often give very useful information about that particular court's procedures. Read them and follow them.

Your Options

The back of your ticket explains your options in depth. The type is so small, though, that few people bother to read it carefully.

Briefly, your options are to plead (1) responsible, (2) responsible with an explanation, or (3) not responsible.

"**Responsible**" means "I did it." If you plead "responsible," you pay the ticket and, if the offense was a moving violation, it will be reported to the secretary of state and points will be assessed. If it is not a violation that must be reported to the secretary of state, the only record of you having the ticket will be with that particular district court.

"**Responsible with an Explanation**" means "I did it, but there were reasons or circumstances for doing it that I want the jurist to be aware of before sentencing." The law allows the jurist to reduce fines and costs because of mitigating circumstances, so, if you use this plea, do not be surprised if you are given a fine.

Russ's Rule for Traffic Court Pleading: If you want the ticket reduced or dismissed, do not plead "responsible with an explanation."

The jurist looks for two things in the explanation. Is there a basis for the "responsible" plea? If not, the matter is set for a hearing. If there is a basis, are there mitigating circumstances?

Because a civil infraction is not a crime, "intent" is not an issue. The jurist presumes that you did not intend to break the traffic law. The only issue they look at is "did you do what you are charged with?"

The law does not specifically allow it, but some jurists dismiss tickets based on letters of explanation they receive. Writing a letter of explanation hoping for a dismissal is a gamble, but you can appeal the responsible plea if you wish. (see "Appeals")

"Not Responsible" means "I did not do it." When this plea is entered, an informal hearing is set unless you ask for a formal hearing.

It is possible that the jurist will reduce your charge if you plead "responsible with an explanation." It is not what the law tells them to do, but there are still jurists who are willing to do what they believe to be the right thing.

A case in point: A young driver took her eyes off the road for a moment. When she looked up, she saw the brake lights glowing on the car ahead of her, slammed on the brakes, and slid on the gravel covered road into the back of the car ahead of her.

A police officer wrote her a ticket for Careless Driving (defined in the Motor Vehicle Code as driving in a manner that is "likely to endanger any person or property, but without wantonness or recklessness").

She appeared before a jurist and pled "responsible with an explanation." The jurist told her that the police department routinely writes traffic crashes as "careless driving" offenses, and reduced the charge to a Violation of the Basic Speed Law (unable to stop in the assured, clear distance ahead).

The young driver thought she was getting a great deal. In a way, she was. The ticket, however, should not have been overwritten. An attorney probably would have argued that the incident did not fit the definition of "careless driving" and it would have been greatly reduced on a plea agreement or she could have been found not responsible for the charged offense.

Since the driver did not take the case to a hearing, she was fortunate that the jurist was willing to deal with a perceived injustice, even though she pled responsible to it.

The better course of action, in my opinion, would be for the jurist to find no basis for the plea and set it for a hearing.

The Worst Option

Not listed on the ticket is a fourth option. This is the "Stick the Ticket in the Glove Box and Hope Everyone Forgets About It" option. This is not an acceptable option, since the courts never forget.

When you choose to ignore the ticket (or forget about it), the court finds you responsible by default and enters a judgment against you.

A notice of default will be mailed to you, telling you how much you owe for the ticket. Notice is also sent to the secretary of state if it is an offense that must be reported.

A Word About Defaults

You default on a civil infraction when you do not appear as scheduled for a court appearance. This can be either for the initial appearance or at any court hearing.

There may be a good reason for not appearing as scheduled, which is why the court sends a notice of the default.

Check the date on the notice *as soon as you get it* because defendants have fourteen days from the date the court sent the default notice to ask that the default be set aside. *It is important to look at the date right away, because a court can prepare the notice on a Thursday, not mail it until Friday after 5:00 P.M., meaning you may not get the notice until Monday or Tuesday. Yet, your 14 days began on the Thursday the notice was generated.*

There is a form that can be used (SCAO form CIA 04), but the motion can be made in writing or in person.

In the motion, explain why you did not appear and that you want to offer a defense or an explanation. You must also include a cash bond (if doing so by mail, check with the court about using a money order or bank draft) equal to the fine and cost judgment. No cash, no hearing on the motion.

The jurist may set aside the default for good cause. Obviously, this is a gamble, since "good cause" is different for each jurist. If the jurist agrees that your excuse is a good one, a hearing will be set.

Sometimes, the informal hearing is heard directly after the motion to set aside the default. When you file your motion, ask the court clerk what that court's practice is.

If you cannot meet the fourteen day standard, you can still ask the court to set aside the default, but the requirements are tougher [see Michigan Court Rule 2.603(D)]. If you miss the fourteen day window and still want to fight the ticket, a trip to an attorney is definitely in order.

The default judgment is a **real** judgment against you. Nasty things can happen to you if you ignore the judgment. Those are covered more fully in **Fail To Appear.**

So you want to have a Hearing

There are two main reasons to go to court with your ticket. Either you did not deserve to get it or you do not want the points on your record.

I Did Not Deserve The Ticket

This is a legitimate reason to go to court. There are many reasons why people believe they did not deserve to get tickets.

There may be mitigating circumstances, like illness, equipment failure, or a family emergency.

Regardless of the reason, if you believe that you do not deserve the ticket you were given, you should fight it.

I Do Not Want The Points

"Points" are the true punishment for a moving violation, haunting drivers and punishing them for three years or more.

Because there are really two sets of points (secretary of state and insurance), the current point system is, in my opinion, an affront to true justice.

The reason some jurists dismiss tickets for first time offenders is because of the inequity in the point system. Only the legislature, though, can make the system right.

One reason *not* to go to court is if you want to complain about the officer. The court is a separate branch of government and a judge cannot discipline a member of the executive branch. Also, the officer is likely to get overtime pay for appearing in court, since most officers are on the road during the afternoon and evening shift and court is held during the day shift. If your case revolves around a complaint about the officer, you may actually be doing the officer a favor by putting more money in his pocket.

A good jurist focuses on the facts in the case, i.e., did you do what the officer says you did. I know there are a few officers on the road who deserve to have complaints filed against them. My courtroom experience, though, showed me that if an officer goes "by the book," he or she appears to be rude. A driver's perception of the traffic stop is clouded by the embarrassment and anger of getting caught. A "Sgt. Joe Friday" handing you the ticket is going to seem very rude under those circumstances.

The best way to deal with an officer complaint is to address it to the chief (local department), sheriff (county), or post commander (state), depending on which department the officer belongs to.

If you want to have a hearing, here are a few recommendations:

Call the Court

Since the ticket says you can call the court, this is a good place to start. You can find out many things with a phone call, like whether or not you can set your hearing date by telephone or by email? (If not, what is the preferred way for the court you are calling?)

Most courts have automated phone systems where, with the press of a button, you can get directions to the court, court hours, and some prices for the more common traffic tickets.

I always recommend, though, that one appears "in person" if possible. Like a ballplayer who visits a new stadium the day before a game, it is important for you to know what your playing field is like.

Make Nice With The Clerks

Appearing in person gives you the opportunity to connect with a court clerk by showing that "you are not such a bad person after all."

People who work in courts, except for jurists, are surrounded by negative people all day. Every case has a winner and a loser and the losers have to go back to the clerks to pay their fines.

People with positive attitudes are a joy to have around.

Because you appear to be a nice, considerate person, the clerk may give you a little extra information. For example, what is the magistrate or judge like? Does the court have a program that can get rid of points, like "under advisement" or "dismissal with costs?" Does the court offer alternative sentencing, like a "safe driving adjournment" or a written essay for youthful first offenders?

That sort of information not only helps you build a strategy, but it is information police officers already know. They can and will use it to their advantage if need be.

The more you know about the field of battle, the better your chance of winning.

Besides getting useful information, you also walked out of the courthouse with a court date and time. *Being at the mercy of the mail is a potential problem. It is not unusual for some courts to send out over 100,000 pieces of mail each year. At least a few of those pieces of mail will get lost and you do not want one of them to be yours.*

You may "appear" in writing to request your court date, but there is a greater chance of having your unopened request sitting on someone's desk at the courthouse. This is a rare event that, again, you do not want to happen to you.

Also, if the court mails a notice, postcards are often used, increasing (in my mind, at least) the likelihood of it getting lost or misplaced.

Can you fax your appearance? Some courts allow you to fax your request. Others will not. *I really like the courts that accept faxed appearances from lawyers, but not from the public. Just another benefit of being in the "club."* Call your specific court for information. Because some courts have web sites (see appendix 3), you may be able to file your appearance by email. The web site will tell you if that option is open.

Questions To Ask The Clerk

Where are the hearings held?

Courtrooms, judge's chambers, and magistrate's offices are all places where informal hearings are held. Formal hearings are always in a courtroom.

This seems like a simple question, and it is. If you know where to go before you walk into the courthouse, it is one less thing you have to worry about on the day of your hearing.

Where and how do I check in for my hearing?

Depending on the court, you may have to check in at the "traffic" counter, the court room, or with the court officer. If you know beforehand, you decrease the risk of missing the hearing because you did not check in properly.

Does the court give individual or group hearing times?

Some courts give each person a different time for their hearing. Usually, these are five to ten minutes apart. Other courts, most, in fact, hold all of that day's hearings at a particular time.

That kind of scheduling is difficult for the ticket holder, because it can mean a long wait.

Depending on which scheduling option your court has, you may want to ask other questions.

If you have your own individual time to appear, ask:

"If I am not on time, how long until I am defaulted?"

When I gave individual times, I allowed fifteen minutes from the scheduled hearing time before I closed the case with the default (defendant did not appear) or dismissal (police officer did not appear). Some courts are less generous, some more.

"Can I pick a date/time that are convenient for me?

Courts may allow you to choose times within reason. Most, however, have particular dates and times where they hear these cases. The bigger the court, the less likely you are to get a date and time that you like.

"Can I watch other hearings?"

Court cases should always be open to the public, but if hearings are held in an office, security and the size of the office may dictate the ability of the public to watch.

Also, the jurist may not want the aggravation caused when one defendant is given a break for a legitimate reason, and the next person in line says "I want what he got!"

If there are group times, you should ask these questions:

"How do you determine who goes first?"

You should know before you go into court how long you will have to wait. It is just plain wrong for a person to have to wait two hours (or even an hour) after the appearance time for a five minute hearing. Even so, make sure you are at the court on time.

There is no law or court rule that requires a jurist to show courtesy in scheduling. One court I am familiar with scheduled hearings at 9:00 AM as a group. At 11:15 AM, the jurist entered the court room and announced that anyone who wanted to pay the costs and have the ticket dismissed should go to the front of the room, give their names, pick up a judgment form, and go to the clerk's window to pay. There were still people in line to pay after noon.

"Where are the Hearings Held?"

As I referred to earlier, your hearing may be held in the courtroom, an office, or the judge's chambers. You may have to stand or you may be allowed to sit. Again, these are little details, but when you step up for your hearing, your thoughts should be on your defense strategy and not side tracked with thoughts like "Where do I stand?" or "Oh my God! I'm in the judge's chambers!"

Chapter 4

Your Hearing

Preparing Your Defense

I know you have the right to represent yourself and that a lawyer cannot represent you at an informal hearing.

I also know that an attorney trained and/or experienced in traffic cases can look at your case, give you an honest assessment and, perhaps, come up with an innovative legal strategy for you to follow.

Russ's First Rule: It is **never** *a bad idea to consult an attorney.*

Consulting an attorney does not mean you have to hire one for your defense. You can often get what you need for the price of an office call.

If the attorney tells you that retaining his services is your only hope, get a second opinion. There are times when a formal hearing with legal representation is advisable. A second opinion will confirm the assessment and give you comparison prices as well.

Buy a Book?

There are a number of books on the market that tell you how to win traffic cases in court.

When I was a magistrate, I read many of these books. They are generally written for people in states, like California, where the court systems are different than Michigan's.

One hazard a person can run into is taking those books so literally that the defendant feels and acts cocky. To the jurist, the defendant comes off looking like he is telling the jurist what the law really means.

Russ's Rule #2: Never Tick Off The Judge!

Making yourself seem smarter than the jurist is never a good idea. A negative first impression makes it unlikely that you will win your case.

I remember a case where an attorney appeared before me as a defendant at an informal hearing. He normally works in corporate law and is a very good trial attorney.

He received a parking ticket and decided to fight it at an informal hearing. He addressed the facts in the case and never tried to show me up, even though, with his experience, he could have. He understood the importance of Rule #2. *(He won the case, although not based on his arguments. My finding was that the signage was improper and, therefore, not binding.)*

Back to the books, they seem to take up a lot of space telling how you can discredit the officer, the radar unit, or both. Experience tells me that both of those strategies are for chumps.

Here are my recommendations. If you want to, as a defense, discredit the officer, hire a lawyer to do it for you. Let the officer hold a grudge against the lawyer, not you.

It will only hurt you to verbally attack an officer in court. Remember that, in most cases, the jurist knows the officer professionally and has an opinion of the officer's credibility. Besides, if the officer said you were belligerent or uncooperative at the stop, it is best to say "I disagree with the officer's assessment, and I will take that issue up at a different time." If you launch into a defensive, emotional tirade about the officer's behavior, it tends to give credibility to the officer's stated assessment of you.

If you want to try to discredit the radar unit, you will have an easier time after you lose your informal hearing. It is almost impossible to beat a radar or laser ticket (see Appendix 2, *Thank You Zolton*). At the informal hearing you will hear the officer's evidence/testimony, allowing you to see any weakness in the case that can be addressed at the formal hearing.

A formal hearing is held before a judge and is treated as if the informal hearing was never held. At the formal hearing, you can concentrate on whatever weakness you may find from the testimony at the informal hearing. Again, an attorney can help a great deal with your defense at that point.

One popular book on beating traffic tickets still tells how to discredit radar units that are calibrated with tuning forks. The last of those units in Michigan, I think, is being used by a security guard at a campground near Port Huron.

My point is that those books are generally not worth the money you spend on them, since the only sure way to beat a ticket is to not get one in the first place.

You're on the air

There are radio programs throughout Michigan on which attorneys dispense free legal advice. Call your local bar association to see if they are aware of any such programs in your area. You can also call around to the radio stations listed in your phone book.

Look up the Law

It is no longer difficult to look up a law. It often takes no more than a trip to your local library. If the library does not have the book you need, an Internet terminal is probably available for you to access a law related web site. If all else fails, each county maintains a public law library.

Local Public Library

Many libraries have copies of Michigan Vehicle Code, The Criminal Code, and The Michigan Court Rules (MCR). These are great for looking up the law itself. For a look at the law *and* related court cases, you will need The Michigan Complied Laws Annotated (MCLA) which is a multi-volume set. The high cost of the updated MCLA (they must be updated annually) makes it unlikely that any but the largest public libraries have them.

Internet

There are a number of law related sites on the Internet where the public can get free access to the latest laws. A list of my favorite sites is located in Appendix 3.

County Public Law Library

Part of the fine paid by traffic violators goes to maintain the law library in your county. These libraries are usually located in the county courthouse. Check with your county clerk for its location and hours of operation.

County law libraries are generally research-only facilities, so do not go expecting to check anything out. The books that will be most helpful to you are:

MCLA

As previously stated, the MCLA follows the text of the law with a list and summary of related court decisions on prior rulings of the circuit, appeals, and supreme courts that help interpret the law.

If you decide to look up the full decision, Appeals Court (Mich App) and Supreme Court (Mich) volumes will be in the county law library. For example, reading the citation (location of the decision) for 34 Mich App 612 (1971), you will find the decision in the 34th volume of Mich App on page 612. It was a 1971 decision of the court. A directory of abbreviations used in the MCLA is located in the front of each volume.

Callahan's Michigan Digest

This volume contains summaries of court decisions on a given topic.

Michigan Bar Journal

The Bar Journal is the monthly magazine published by the Michigan Bar Association for its members. If the Bar Journal has covered the area of the law you are working on, it may contain some helpful information.

Using Exhibits

Your hearing will probably take place weeks away from the time you received the ticket. In that time, leaves may grow or fall. Skid marks disappear. Signs may sprout where none existed. Therefore, it is important that you gather evidence as soon as possible. After the stop, as soon as possible afterward, write a narrative of what happened, including any direct quotes from the officer. Be specific. Use as much detail as you can. It will help you remember when the time comes. The officer will document the stop with notes right after delivering the ticket to you. You should do the same. Notes not written right away will not carry the same weight.

Photographs are sometimes helpful, but the lens you use may distort distances. Video is often better evidence because the perspective can be changed to give far away, close up, and normal views.

Make sure that you make arrangements with the court no later than a week before your hearing to have a video tape player, easel, or whatever else you may need. If the court cannot provide the items you need, it gives you time to make other arrangements.

Remember to keep the exhibits *relevant* to your defense.

Get to the Point

I cannot stress enough the importance of getting to the point of your defense. An interesting or well reasoned argument usually catches the jurist's attention.

Perspective, perspective, perspective

A traffic hearing is not necessarily "He said/She said." It is more like "He saw/She saw."

After the jurist hears the story of events from the officer's perspective, you tell the story from your perspective. The officer must tell about the traffic stop (and will probably relate parts of your conversation with him/her) to show that you were the person he gave the ticket to. Sometimes your perspective of the actual stop should be addressed at the hearing. That is a question to ask your attorney.

In giving his account of events at the stop, the officer may make what you consider to be a false, personal attack upon you. This may or may not be the case. He may be trying to rattle you. Then, again, it may be the officer's true perception of events.

If you must respond to the "attack," consider a response like "I strongly disagree with the officer's description of my behavior, but I can address that with his chief/ the sheriff/ his lieutenant."

Then start your defense.

Rehearse

Practice your presentation. Think of it as a speech before an audience of one. Practice your presentation in front of someone you know. Encourage questions. Make sure your argument makes sense to the person you tell it to.

Adjournments

It is possible that you can request an adjournment by telephone. Even if the court allows it, remember that there is no record of your request. If the clerk is busy and forgets your request, you could be out of luck.

If the court requires your request to be in writing, ask if you can fax or e-mail the request. (All courts in Michigan have e-mail addresses. Whether or not they use it for public communication is at the discretion of each court. If the court has a web site, it is possible they have a separate public e-mail account.)

Most courts have drop boxes for after-hours payments. You can put your written request in the drop box if you are unable to make it during regular business hours. *(You may want to follow up by telephone if you use the drop box option.)*

Don't Wait Until the Last Minute

Courts often are not inclined to give last minute adjournments unless there is an emergency that keeps you from appearing. Forgetfulness and oversleeping are not emergencies, making it a true case of "if you snooze, you lose."

On the Day of the Hearing

Be On Time

As stated earlier, the court does not have to give you an adjournment or extra time to appear.

If the court has a "cattle call" appearance time (everyone scheduled for the same time), appearing early could mean that your case is heard earlier. (Then again, they may take cases alphabetically. That is why it is a good idea to ask.)

If you were given a specific time to appear, the court may grant a window of up to 15 minutes in which you can appear before being defaulted. (Again, these are informal windows, so if the jurist has an appointment to keep, you may be held directly to the hearing time.)

Remember, if you do not appear on time, you lose by default. If the officer does not appear, the court may either adjourn or dismiss the case against you.

Waiting

Always be prepared to wait. If you are lucky, the jurist assigned to hear your case will be on time and try to keep the cases moving quickly and efficiently. More likely, though, on the day of *your* hearing, the jurist will arrive late, spend time on personal business in chambers, or take a long lunch. If you have a scheduled court date, your file should be ready. This is, however, not always the case. Staff inefficiency or judicial meddling in the administration can cause files to be misplaced or simply not ready when court opens for business on your court date.

Spend Your Time Wisely

Talk to the officer. The time before the hearing is your time to play "Let's Make A Deal." Ask the officer if it is possible for you to plead responsible to a no-point violation. "Impeding Traffic" is a common one to plea to, since it carries a reasonable fine and is not reported to the secretary of state. If you have no points on your record, it is more likely you will get a deal. Remember, too, that there are no guarantees. If the officer received a negative impression of you at the stop, a deal is unlikely. It is also possible that the officer or her department has a "no deals" policy. Those policies are not common, but they exist.

Be Ready for the Worst

Part of preparing for the hearing is knowing what will happen if you lose. The law gives you seven days in which to appeal a decision against you. Knowing the deck is stacked against you, decide your post-hearing action *before* the hearing. For example, if you lose the hearing, is the increase in your insurance rates enough to justify an appeal? If so, bring with you the cash to pay your appeal bond, which is equal to the amount of the judgment ordered by the jurist.

The Hearing

Here is a rough sketch of what will happen when the jurist calls your name for the informal hearing.

Your case file will contain, at minimum, the original traffic ticket. It may also contain a copy of correspondence you sent to or received from the court, and a copy of your driving record.

The driving record should not be reviewed before the hearing. This avoids a prejudiced jurist. I required the police officer to run the driving record and keep it until I asked for it. I know of many jurists who have the same policy because it is too easy for the jurist to take a peek.

Michigan law requires district court magistrates to go through a training session before being certified to conduct informal hearings. According to that training, the jurist, after "calling the case," i.e., asking the officer, defendant, and witnesses to come forward, may briefly explain the proceedings. You will then know who will testify first, and what the jurist's ground rules are.

The charge will be read and you will be asked if you understand the charge. Do not confuse "understand the charge" with "agree with the charge" or "understand why you were charged." There are few ways that will ruin your credibility quicker than to answer "No" when you know darn well what it means to drive through a red light.

The jurist will administer an oath to all participants in your hearing.

The police officer is supposed to present his case first. In reality, this practice varies from court to court. I once heard a jurist begin a hearing by asking the defendant "Well, what did you do?" *(I should add that this person was also one of the fairest jurists I ever met and that I know of no one who did not get a fair hearing.)*

The officer gives the first account because he must establish that a particular section of the Michigan Vehicle Code was violated and that you violated it.

If the jurist asks you to go first, give your defense. It does no good to argue procedure, since jurists run their own courtrooms and may take offense to someone who acts as if they are more knowledgeable about how to run a courtroom than they are.

The jurist may need to clarify some facts after the initial testimony. Then, the jurist may give you an opportunity to question the officer so that you can clarify certain points.

If so, remember that questions (1) should be directed to the jurist (e.g., "I would like to ask the officer if his radar unit was attached to the vehicle."), (2) should not be argumentative (you will have a chance to give your own testimony later), and (3) should be relevant to the case.

Then it is your turn.

After your testimony, the officer may have an opportunity to question you. The same rules of questioning will apply to the officer.

The jurist will make a decision after the testimony is taken. Hopefully, the reasons for the decision will be explained to you.

Common Courtroom Mistakes

Here are some common mistakes that citizens make during their hearings.

Argue about minute details

Everyone makes mistakes, even an officer writing a road side ticket on a dark, rainy night. If an officer mistakes a black car for one that is dark blue or dark green, it is understandable.

Arguing that "It wasn't me."

If you use that argument, the first question the jurist will ask is probably "Then how did you find out about this ticket?"

You should probably not use that argument if the officer handed you the ticket at the roadside.

Using "Sir" or "Your Honor" too much

Well placed, these words convey respect. Used to too often, they are patronizing or condescending.

Improper Courtroom Attire-Hats

Wearing a hat or baseball cap in the courtroom shows disrespect to the jurist. I have witnessed jurists become visibly irritated when a hat-wearing defendant appeared in front of them. Wear one at your peril.

Improper Courtroom Attire—General

You want to convey to the jurist that you respect the legal system. Wear clothing that conveys that message. These days, it is not necessary to wear a suit, skirt, or tie, but shirts with slogans are unwise.

I will never forget a defendant who appeared before me for arraignment, arrested the previous night for domestic violence. He was hung over, wore his T-shirt inside out and had his hands cuffed in front of him. He kept his hands up to hide the art work on the shirt, but it was still visible. It showed a large hand, middle finger extended with the words "F—Y—" emblazoned above it. He was terrified at having to appear before a jurist dressed that way. At least he had the good sense to try to cover it.

Sanctions

If the jurist finds the defendant responsible, sanctions are imposed. Sanctions are supposed to be high enough to discourage risky driving. Sanctions are usually referred to as "fines," but the fine is only a small part of the sanctions.

This is the part of the hearing where the jurist should review the driving record. A good driving record could, but seldom does, mean lower sanctions. A bad record could mean more.

When you call the court and ask for the amount of the "fine" on a civil infraction charge, the clerk actually tells you the total of the fine, court costs, and fees.

Fine: This is a civil fine. If a state law was violated, the fine must go to the county public and law libraries. If a local ordinance was violated, 1/3 of the fine goes to the political subdivision whose ordinance was violated, and 2/3 to whatever political entity funds the court (usually the county).

Court Costs: At least $5.00 of the sanction will be court costs. These costs are assessed to offset the cost to the funding unit connected with prosecuting the civil infraction. Costs are paid to the district court's funding unit, except when a local ordinance is violated. Then, 1/3 of the costs go to the community whose law was violated.

Fees: Out of each moving traffic civil infraction sanction, $5.00 is sent to the Highway Safety Fund, $5.00 to Secondary Road Patrol and Training Fund, $5.00 to the Michigan Justice Training Fund, and $9.00 State Costs, most of which goes toward the judicial and legislative retirement programs.

Rehabilitation: The court can also order you to complete a driver safety class or other education, treatment, or rehabilitation program, although you cannot be placed on probation to allow the court to monitor your compliance. These programs carry costs separate from the fines and costs the court orders you to pay.

This whole business of where the money goes is confusing and boring, but since you are paying the money, you deserve to know where it goes.

A Word About Points

If you are found responsible for a moving violation, the secretary of state adds points to your driving record. When your insurance company looks at your driving record and notes a new offense, points are added to your insurance record. The number of points assessed are based on how much of a "risk" that offense carries.

For example, driving 6 mph over the speed limit on an interstate highway is less of a risk (1 point) than driving 6 mph over the speed limit on a two lane highway (2 points), as far as the secretary of state is concerned. The risk is a traffic safety risk. The insurance points also reflect a traffic safety risk, but more as it relates to insurance payoffs.

Here is a list of some secretary of state point totals:

OUIL	6
OWI	4
Reckless Driving	6
Careless Driving	3
Freeway Speed 1-5 over	0
Freeway Speed 6-10 over	1
Freeway Speed 11-15 over	2
Freeway Speed 16- 25 over	3
Freeway Speed 26+ over	4
Speeding 1-10 over	2
Speeding 11-15 over	3

Speeding 16 over	4
Disobeying a Stop Sign or Signal	3
Improper Passing	3
All other moving violations	2
Defective Equipment	0
Wide Load	0
Seat Belt	0

Insurance company points (commonly called "insurance eligibility points") are a different matter. There is not state law telling insurance companies what they can charge. Each company calculates a driver's risk factors differently.

Risk factors used include the age and experience of the driver, points on the driver's record, accidents, and insurance payouts.

MCL 500.2103 (4) outlines the insurance eligibility point system for moving violations:

Speeding 10 mph or less	2
Speeding 11-15 mph over	3
Speeding 16 mph and over	4
Freeway Speed 1-15 mph over	2
All other moving violations	2
First Accident (over 50% at fault)	3
2+ Accidents (over 50% at fault)	4

The time limit for losing insurance eligibility points is different, too. The secretary of state points stay on a record for two years from the date when the plea or finding of responsible is made, even though the offense itself stays on for seven years. *(Alcohol offenses stay on for ten years).*

Insurance companies, however, look at moving violations during the three years before your policy is renewed. For example, if I was found responsible for a speeding ticket on June 1, 1996, those points would drop off my driving record on June 1, 1998. If my insurance was up for renewal on May 25, 1999, the insurance company would add insurance points for that 1996 ticket.

Waiving Fines and Costs

Waiving fines and costs is not the same as dismissing the ticket.

Defective equipment, No Proof of Insurance, No Registration, and Child Restraint Violations are what are often called "dismissable" offenses. This means that if you fix the defect, show that your insurance was valid or the registration was in effect at the time of the stop, or you purchased a child safety seat and show proof before the appearance date on the ticket, the fines and costs "shall" be waived.

In other words, the ticket stays on your record, but you do not have to pay the fines and costs.

Practices differ, however, to court to court. Some courts simply dismiss the ticket. On the other extreme, I know of one jurist who regularly refused to waive fines and costs for child restraint violations because the jurist thought it too serious an offense to waive the fines and costs. The practice in that court may have since changed. But when citizens do not know the law, it makes it easier for judges to, essentially, break the law or make their own law, in their own courtroom.

Before the appearance date on your ticket, make sure you know what your court's practice is.

After The Hearing-More Waiting

When the hearing is over, you will probably have to wait some more. If you win the case, you can simply walk out the front door. *Some courts give a copy of the judgment. Many do not. If you want a copy and it is not offered to you, just ask for it.*

If you lose, though, you have to pay your fine or the appeal bond.

In some courts, you can take the judgment form to the cashier and pay. In other courts, you must wait for the paperwork to go from the courtroom to the cashier before you pay. This takes time. Maybe a long time. Be prepared to wait.

Appeals

If you are unhappy with the jurist's decision, you have the right to appeal it. There are restrictions, though.

If you wish to appeal the decision of the informal hearing, the next step will be a formal hearing. To appeal, you must pay a cash bond in the amount of the judgment within seven days of that judgment.

The court may or may not be able to schedule your formal hearing date at the time you file the appeal. If not, watch your mailbox and call the court's scheduling clerk back within a week of posting the bond. Keep calling at weekly intervals until you have your court date.

If you wish to appeal the decision of your formal hearing, the new hearing will take place in the Circuit Court. The appeal must be filed there.

If you wish to appeal your default judgment, the appeal must be made by paying a cash bond in the amount of the judgment. That amount is always the price of the ticket. The bond must be paid within fourteen days of the default judgment.

The key words to remember when it comes to appeals are **cash bond** and **time limit**.

Formal Hearing

A formal hearing is just what the name implies. Forget the Judge's chambers, you are now in the center ring.

The formal hearing is held in a courtroom. The judge wears a robe and looks down on you from above.

Every word is recorded. The prosecuting attorney, or maybe an assistant prosecutor, represents the police officer. An attorney can represent you, if you like.

Other than the outward formality, the hearings themselves do not differ greatly in content from the informal hearing. They still turn on a preponderance of the evidence and the judge treats them as if the informal hearing did not happen.

You may find it easier to negotiate a plea agreement before your formal hearing. The reason is in the personalities involved. (Remember that I am speaking in generalities.)

Police officers are a proud bunch. If they lose a case, it means they were wrong. Police officers do not want to be wrong.

Prosecutors, on the other hand, are a step removed from the ticket. They want to win, but as long as they get a plea of "responsible" or "guilty" to *something*, they win.

One more thing to remember about prosecutors: if you are the defendant, the prosecutor is not your friend regardless of how friendly he/she seems. The prosecutor's job is to win the case. The case *against* you. They may lull you into thinking they are doing you a favor, but be careful.

A trip to an attorney before your formal hearing can help you a great deal, even if you do not retain him or her.

Chapter 5

Misdemeanors

A misdemeanor is a violation of any law where punishment includes incarceration of up to one year and/or a fine. (When the jurist says the offense includes a possible fine amount, it is misleading, since court costs and fees are always added if fines are ordered. The extra costs usually double the fine amount.)

If someone says "It is just a misdemeanor," they refer to the garden variety offense where the possible maximum penalty is 90 days in jail and/or $100 in fines. These are often referred to as "simple" or "90-day" misdemeanors.

In legal circles, however, a "minor offense" often means an offense carrying a possible maximum penalty of up to 92 days in jail and/or $500 in fines. For these minor offenses, Appearance Tickets are issued. If the offense carries a possible maximum jail sentence of 93 days or more, a Complaint will be issued by the prosecuting attorney.

Most violations of the Motor Vehicle Code are simple misdemeanors unless they are specifically listed as civil infractions or if a harsher penalty is listed.

Probable Cause

A term often used in the legal system is "probable cause." It is a standard jurists use to decide if a search or arrest warrant is issued or to send a felony case to the circuit court for possible trial.

The Michigan Court of Appeals, in 1981, defined probable cause as "where the facts and circumstances presented [by the police officer or prosecutor to the jurist] would warrant a man of reasonable caution to believe that the items sought to be seized were in the stated place."

In other words, based on the information presented, would a reasonable person, a "fair minded person of average intelligence," believe the allegation to be true. [People v Ward, 226 Mich 45; 196 NW 971 (1924)]

Arraignment

The arraignment is the defendant's first appearance in court. Blackstone wrote about arraignment procedures in his commentaries on the English common law and the general procedure remains the same.

Simply put, the arraignment is where the accused is formally notified of the charge, the possible penalties, his/her rights in court, and is given the opportunity to enter a plea. If necessary, bond is also set.

A jurist must be available to conduct arraignments (or set bond) every day of the year. This allows a person taken into custody to have a bond set within one day of the arrest.

At arraignment, the jurist must inform the accused of:

—the name of the offense

—the possible maximum penalty (and the mandatory minimum penalty, if there is one)

—the right to have an attorney represent him/her at all subsequent court proceedings and, if qualified, to have that attorney at public expense. The defendant, however, may have to repay all or part of the attorney fees.

—The right to have a trial heard by a jury or, if the defendant chooses, by the judge.

—The right to be released on bond.

A Word About Court Appointed Attorneys...

A person qualifies for a court appointed attorney if he/she is indigent. What does that mean? A basic financial inability to retain an attorney.

Most courts allow an applicant to fill out a form outlining current employment, earnings, debt, ownership of real property and other major assets, and whether the defendant is qualified for and/or receiving public assistance of any kind.

Most courts will not appoint counsel if the offense is a 90-day misdemeanor, since the defendant is unlikely to spend any time in jail. The courts will generally appoint attorneys on request (although if you are gainfully employed, you may have to repay the attorney costs) if the offense carries a possible maximum penalty of 93 days or more, a minimum jail sentence on conviction, or if the jurist believes the defendant may spend some time in jail.

Bond

The jurist, to be sure the defendant appears at all additional court proceedings, sets an amount of bail.

Bail can be a personal recognizance (taking the defendant's word that he will appear), a secured bond (usually from a bail bondsman), a straight cash amount, or a "ten percent" bail (requires posting only ten percent of the total cash amount ordered by the jurist).

In posting the bail, a bond is created. The bond is a contract, of sorts, between the defendant and the court. If the bail is posted by someone other than the defendant, they are also part of the contract.

In setting the bail, the jurist considers how serious the offense is, the defendant's prior record with the courts, the likelihood of appearing in court, and the potential danger to the public if that person is released. For these purposes, the public can be a single person or the general public at large.

Most jurists attach conditions to bail bonds. For example, since alcohol and illegal drugs are contributing factors to many crimes, jurists commonly order defendants not to possess or consume alcohol or illegal drugs.

The important thing to note about bail is that it is not to be excessive and it is not to be used as punishment.

Prosecutors and police officers are, by nature of their positions, adversarial to defendants. They will often, therefore, request a money bail when only a personal recognizance is necessary.

Politics often enters into bail bond decisions. Prosecutors and jurists must be elected and the "kiss of death" is to be accused of being soft on criminals. It would be unnatural of them to not think, at some level, about how a bond they set on a high profile defendant would look in the morning paper.

How An Arraignment Sounds

The arraignment, as stated, is pretty straightforward. Here is the "script" I used. The name used here is fictitious.

Jurist: *This is case number B96-1234, The People versus Joseph Schmuck. Are you Mr. Schmuck?* (Hopefully, he answers "yes." If he says "no," this could get interesting.)

J: *Mr. Schmuck, you are charged with driving your vehicle on Hadley Road in Metamora Township on April 1, 1996 while your registration plates were not valid. Do you understand what you are being charged with?*

Schmuck: *Yes.*

J: *The possible maximum penalty, if you are found "Guilty," is 90 days in jail and/or $100 in fines, plus court costs. Do you understand?*

S: *Yes.*

J: *You have the right to remain silent. Anything you say, orally or in writing, can be used against you in court. Do you understand?*

S: *Yes.*

J: *You have the right to have an attorney represent you at all additional court proceedings, including at any hearing where you decide to plead "guilty." If you cannot afford to hire an attorney, and you are eligible, the court will appoint one for you. You may, however, be required to repay all or part of those attorney fees. Do you understand your right to have a lawyer?*

S: *Yes.*

J: *Do you wish to be represented by a lawyer in this matter?*

S: *Not at this time.*

J: *If you wish to apply for a court appointed attorney, we will make the application available to you before you leave the courtroom. Do you wish to have an application at this time?*

S: *Not at this time, Your Honor.*

J: *You have the right to have a trial and to have that trial heard by a judge or a jury. At trial, you have the right to confront witnesses against you and to question them under oath. You also have the right to be presumed innocent until proven guilty beyond a reasonable doubt. Do you understand those rights?*

S: *Yes.*

J: *How do you plead to this charge?*

If the defendant pleads Not Guilty, or if the jurist enters a Not Guilty plea on the defendant's behalf, the court sets the date for a Pre-Trial Conference and bail is set.

If the defendant pleads Guilty, the jurist asks a few more questions to ensure that he really wants to plead Guilty.

J: *Do you understand that by pleading guilty, you give up your right to a trial as well as all the rights that accompany a trial?*

S: *Yes.*

J: *Do you understand that by pleading guilty, you give up all the rights I told you about earlier, including your right to have an attorney represent you when you make your plea?*

S: *Yes.*

J: *And you give up that right?*

S: *Yes.*

J: *Did anyone promise you anything in exchange for your guilty plea?*

S: *No.*

J: *Are you doing so freely and voluntarily?*

S: *Yes.*

J: *What did you do to be guilty of this offense?*

If the jurist is satisfied with the defendant's version of events, the plea will be accepted. If not, the plea will not be accepted and the matter will be set for Pre-Trial.

Let's Get This Over With!

It is not uncommon, at arraignment, to hear a defendant say something like, "I did not do it, but I cannot afford to take time off work to fight it."

Who can argue with that? Especially when it usually takes longer to get into your court "appointment" than to get into your doctor's appointment. And people can take sick time to go to the doctor.

When, however, a person is presumed to be innocent, guilt is not something to be dispensed as a convenience. If nothing else, guilt, in court, translates into a loss of freedom. Today, you may only lose the freedom to spend some of your money the way you want to. In the future, if you are unfortunate enough to go to court again as a defendant, you may lose your physical freedom by going to jail.

If The Court Accepts The Guilty Plea

On most simple (90 days and/or $500 in fines) misdemeanors, jurists sentence defendants at arraignment. Remember that magistrates can sentence a person to serve jail time on a 90-day misdemeanor.

Russ's Rule #3: Any time you go before a judge, anything can happen.

Most courts have their own informal sentencing guidelines. For example, a guy receives a ticket for playing his car's radio too loudly in a downtown area, which is a noise ordinance violation carrying a penalty of 90 days in jail and/or $500 in fines. He pleads guilty and the court accepts the plea.

Will he go to jail?

The answer, of course, depends on whether or not the jurist lives in an area where loud car music regularly disturbs his/her domestic tranquillity. The real answer, though, is that it is unlikely, since most jails are already overcrowded.

Will he be forced to listen to Wayne Newton records (or, if a second offense, to John Tesh)? Also unlikely, since it has already been tried and, depending on one's point of view, failed. What is left?

Oh! Yes! The court must operate. The funding unit needs money. Therefore, the sentence will likely be fines and costs of $50 to $100.

Remember, I must write in generalities because every jurist treats every case differently, even in the same courthouse. Some jurists take the path of least resistance. A few try to be creative.

I always applaud creative sentences if I believe them to be just. Fines and costs do not deter future criminal behavior, so the judges might as well be creative in their sentencing.

Be Prepared To Pay

Always come to the courthouse on your arraignment and/or sentencing day with enough cash to cover the maximum monetary penalty.

Courts expect you to pay at sentencing. Michigan law states that a person determined to be responsible must pay at sentencing unless the jurist allows other arrangements. One of the questions you should ask a clerk is about the normal range of sanctions for the offense you are charged with. Bring that amount with you so you can answer "yes" when the jurist asks "Can you pay that today?"

Even though judges often give extra time to pay, I recommend paying right away. The sooner you get out of the clutches of the court, the better it is for you.

Some jurists place defendants on probation until their sanctions are paid off. Probation, and the loss of freedom it brings, is a high price to pay for the privilege of financing your fines and costs through the court.

Pre-Sentence Investigations

Sometimes, depending on the offense, the jurist needs more information in order to issue an appropriate sentence. A pre-sentence investigation report, or PSI, is ordered.

These are normally ordered in more serious cases, like assault or drug crimes, but they can sometimes be useful for lesser offenses.

The PSI is normally conducted by a probation officer, who takes information on the defendant's personal, educational, employment, and court histories and weave them into a narrative that gives the jurist a fuller picture of the defendant and what kind of sanction may help put him back on the straight and narrow.

This, by the way, is one of those times when a plea of guilty a few years earlier, made because the person did not want to take time off from work, can come back to cause the defendant legal harm. The judge will see that conviction under the "court history" heading.

If the jurist orders a PSI, it is not necessarily bad news. However, between the pre-sentence interview and sentencing, it may be advisable to visit an attorney.

Probation

I will not dwell long on probation. If your sentence includes time on probation, your probation officer will tell you everything you need to know. I will, however, offer a few insights.

What Is Probation?

In the strictly legal sense, probation is an alternative to going to jail. It is as if the jurist is saying "I could send you to jail for this offense, but I want to give you the chance to redeem yourself. If you are good for the next six months, I will not have to put you in jail."

"Being good" means complying with all of the judge's orders in the case, including those in the probation order.

In real terms, district court probation is used for general oversight. Most district court probation officers in Michigan average between 200 and 500 cases at any given time, which is more than can possibly be supervised properly each month. Therefore, the probation officer makes sure the classes are attended, fines and costs are paid, and the probationer does not get back into trouble.

If the judge's orders are not complied with, another trip in front of the judge, for a violation hearing, is in order.

Understanding The Probation Order

Every district court probation order has some standard provisions, including that the defendant not leave the state without the court's permission or break any criminal laws and must report to the probation officer as often as the PO requires. The defendant must also pay the fines and costs, which now include probation oversight fees.

After the standard requirements, the probation order lists the sanctions specific to your probation. Like a bond order, these can cover a wide range of items restricted only by the judge's creativity.

One popular provision that has nearly become standard is for the defendant to refrain from possessing or using alcohol or illegal drugs. The thought, which my experience in the system leads me to believe is true, is that alcohol is a contributing factor to many, if not most, crimes. If, therefore, the use of alcohol or drugs is stopped, the probationer may be able to stay out of trouble.

Take, for example, an assaultive crime, like domestic violence. In most cases that came to the attention of the courts I was involved with, the defendant was consuming alcohol or illegal drugs when the crime occurred. During the course of the evening, a topic of conversation came up which, fueled by alcohol, got blown out of proportion. The restraint that a person might have while sober is lost in the flood of a high blood alcohol level. The result is violence.

Don't believe me? Watch *COPS*.

Not Guilty Plea

If a Not Guilty plea is entered by the defendant or if the jurist does not accept a guilty plea, a Not Guilty plea is entered into the record. The defendant's next court date will be a Pre-Trial Conference, commonly called a "Pre-Trial." That is a time set aside to try and resolve the case (i.e., get the defendant to plead guilty to something) before going to the time and expense of a trial.

Specific procedures differ from court to court, but if you go for a pre-trial, you can generally expect to find the same thing.

A prosecuting attorney sits in an office or room in the courthouse with a stack of files, one of which is yours. The prosecutor calls your name and you enter the room. If you have an attorney, you will probably be among the first defendants called. For defense attorneys, time is money and prosecutors and judges try to accommodate them as much as possible and send them on their way to work on other cases. Also, if your attorney is standing around the courthouse with nothing to do but wait for your case, you are being charged dearly for that time. The judges and prosecutors, therefore, are also trying to help you save a few bucks.

Once in the room with the prosecutor, it is time to play "Let's Make A Deal." If the two sides come to an agreement, the plea agreement goes to the judge.

In the courtroom, the judge asks you (and your attorney, if you have one) if you understand what you are pleading to, and that by agreeing to plead guilty to the charge, you give up your right to a trial, etc.

If satisfied, the judge accepts the plea and sentencing is either immediate or set for another day.

If you do not come to a plea agreement, the judge is notified and a trial date is set.

There will still be time before trial for plea bargaining, so if you do not like the deal being offered to you, do not take it.

I offer a word of advice, though. If you decide not to take the plea agreement and do not have an attorney representing you, go talk to one and strongly consider having one represent you at trial.

Lawyers are trained to argue in court. That is what they are supposed to do best. The prosecutor assigned to your case is determined to win and will come to trial well prepared. You should be, too. A defense attorney can even your playing field.

Chapter 6

Small Claims

In many ways, small claims cases are little different than traffic court hearings. They are less formal than the "major" cases, due to the lesser amount of money involved.

Do not let the perceived informality fool you, though. The winner in a small claims case is the person who has "the law" on their side. What is "just" and "right" has comparatively little to do with the outcome.

In exchange for this simple remedy, you must give up certain rights. *The courts have a more friendly way of saying it. To the legal system, you "waive" your rights. It sounds less drastic.*

Here are the rights you give up for the convenience of a small claims hearing: 1) attorney, 2) jury trial, and 3) right of appeal.

These are pretty significant rights to give up, but it may not make sense for you to spend $1,000 on a lawyer to collect $500.

Remember that you are asked to give up rights, not arbitrary rules. You do not have to give up those rights and neither does the other party. If you choose not to give up those rights, the case is moved to what is commonly called a "general civil" case. A pre-trial conference will be scheduled.

One more thing. If the other party wants the case to go to general civil, you should see an attorney. Rest assured, the other side will have one.

Filing The Case

Before filing the case, call the courthouse to find out what it will cost. You will have to pay the filing fee and the cost of service by certified mail, if that is how the papers will be served. If you choose personal service, you may have to pay those costs up front, too, depending on the court and who serves the papers.

A Note About Service: If you are a party to a suit, you cannot serve the papers yourself. Other than that restriction, just about anyone else can do it for you.

You will need certain information to properly file the case.

Name: This should go without saying. Unfortunately, I still have to say it. If you are suing a corporation or someone doing business under an assumed name (DBA), make sure you have that information.

For example, if Joe Schmuck is doing business as Schmuck's Widgets, take that information with you when you file the case. DBA information is available from your local county clerk's office.

If it is a corporation, you must list a "resident agent," or someone who can speak for the company in the case. *(A corporation is nothing more than words on paper. It is difficult to serve pleadings on a stack of papers and even harder to get it to respond.)* Ask the court clerk where you can call to get resident agent information.

Address: The papers have to go somewhere and since they are served either by certified mail or by personal service, a correct address is necessary.

If the address is wrong, the papers are not served. The case will be postponed until the papers can be served.

Where Do You File?

You must file the case in the district court of the judicial district where the defendant lives, the business that is being sued is located, or where the cause of action occurred.

If you file the case in the wrong court, the case will either be dismissed or transferred. Either way, it means delays and, possibly, more filing fees.

Forms

SCAO Form DC84 is required to start small claims actions. These forms are available at your district court's civil division counter. There will be a small charge for the form. If you need help filling it out, ask for it. The law requires the clerk to help with DC 84 on request. (MCL 600.8403)

Witnesses

If you have witnesses, ask them if they will attend the hearing and help you out. If they will not come voluntarily, they can be ordered by the court to testify through a subpoena. Your court's civil clerks have the forms and the clerk or the jurist can sign it.

You will probably pay about a quarter for the subpoena form, but the courts cannot charge any other subpoena fees. You, however, will be responsible for paying a witness fee to everyone you subpoena. Those fees are $6.50 for a half day and $13.00 for a full day, along with $.10 per mile for the witness's round trip to court.

You are also responsible for arranging to have the subpoenas served.

If you win your case, the court may order the other party to pay your witness costs.

Preparing Your Small Claims Case

These are not TV Judges

"The People's Court" television show paved the way for the current crop of "reality" judge shows. Judge Joseph Wapner handled his television courtroom with dignity, the way one would want a courtroom to be handled. The same cannot be said of most of the others on television today.

With Judge Wapner's court, the litigants and their cases made the entertainment. Today, the judges are as much a part of the show as the litigants. If a judge ever talked to me the way those TV judges do, I would be on the complaint line to the Michigan Judicial Tenure Commission in a heartbeat.

What I am trying to say is, it is not wise to prepare for your case by watching Judge Hoozit's TV show.

Sit in on your court's small claims court

As is the case with traffic court, find out when the jurist assigned to your case has hearings and watch. Take notes. (Try not to be the last one there. Some jurists will ask, from the bench, why you are there. It can be an awkward moment)

You can learn much about the jurist's temperament and how cases are decided. You can see successful litigants and what makes them so.

Jurists handle their courtrooms differently, depending on their individual personalities. Therefore, observation is the key to getting an edge when your case is called.

As with traffic court, watch the cases ahead of time. Do not wait until the day of your hearing and watch the few cases ahead of yours. You have enough to think about without trying to cover an entire last minute strategy. Besides, the courtroom itself can be intimidating and you need time to get used to those august surroundings.

Not to mention that your case could be the first one called.

Preparing your case

There are books that go into greater depth on how to prepare your small claims case. That, to me, borders on legal advice and I will defer that advice to others.

I will offer some tips that, though important, are not all-inclusive.

Document! Document! Document!

Keep receipts. Keep journals of discussions. Pictures, diagrams and anything else that can strengthen your case is important.

Jurists like to look at things that help them make the decision. Yes, the proof really is in the pudding.

Russ's Rule #4: The difference between "he said" and "she said" is good documentation.

No personal attacks

If the other guy wants to call you a "lame brained so-and-so," let him. The jurist will take note of the litigants' temperaments. Your focus is to win the case. Stay focused on...

Just The Facts

As commonly used, a "fact" is something that is true. In the language of the law, both sides enter "facts" into evidence, meaning that not all of the facts are true.

One fact may, in reality, be true. The other may be a person's perception of the truth. The jurist determines the truth, which is why judges are called "finders of fact."

You must make sure that your facts are relevant to your case. Keep things simple enough for the jurist to follow.

Review the section on Traffic Hearings

A court hearing is a court hearing. Some basic principles apply regardless of what kind of hearing you are going in for.

The specifics are different, though, so do not attend a morning of traffic hearings and expect to be prepared for a small claims case.

Russ's Rule #5: Preparation Helps You Win Cases

Settling The Case

Cases are often settled before the hearing. Very often, the act of filing a lawsuit is enough of a catalyst to get both sides talking seriously to each other.

Community Dispute Resolution is being used by more and more courts to try and get pre-hearing settlements. These arbitrators have a good track record of getting the sides to settle.

If the two sides come together, a consent agreement is signed by the judge assigned to the case and by both parties to the suit, making the agreement binding.

Appeals

Can you appeal a small claims decision? Yes and No.

If the case was heard by a magistrate, you have seven days in which to appeal the decision. The appeal will be heard by a district judge.

If a judge hears the case, the decision is final. You do not have a right to appeal the small claims decision to a higher court.

Collecting The Judgment

I cannot begin to count the number of times someone told me they would not initiate a small claims case because they would not be able to collect the money judgment.

Nonsense!

Small claims judgments are collectible. Sometimes, they take a little work. I figure, if it is important enough to go to court, it is important enough to collect the money.

Here is a quick look at some ways to collect small claims judgments. (You should check with your local district court, or on line at a court web site. There is a free pamphlet called *Collecting Money From A Small Claims Judgment* that goes into greater detail about collecting your judgment. Ask for a copy after your small claims hearing so you have time to prepare, if necessary.

The best deal is if the defendant can pay you right away. This is seldom the case, though. If the defendant cannot pay, set up a payment schedule, in court, with the judge or magistrate.

If you win your case by default, the court will mail a copy of the judgment to the defendant. Within 30 days, the defendant must either pay the judgment or file form DC 87, *Affidavit of Judgment Debtor*, which tells the defendant's workplace and bank accounts.

If the defendant still does not pay, things get a little complicated. Your choices are now garnishment (collecting directly from the wages or bank accounts) or an execution (a court officer seizes the defendant's property and sells it to pay the judgment). You must wait at least 21 days after the judgment is signed before starting either process.

For the latter, you will need form DC 19, *Execution against Property*. You must know where the defendant lives and works, the assets that can be seized and sold and their locations, and other information that describes the defendant and his property. If you do not have that information, you will have to go through a process called "discovery."

Your first step is to file a discovery subpoena and an *Affidavit for Judgment Debtor Examination*. The court will give you a date and time to put on the form (MC 11, *Subpoena (Order to Appear)*). The subpoena, once signed by the judge, orders the defendant to appear and be questioned.

Yes, there are filing fees for all of these "post judgment" actions. The court clerk will tell you what those fees are.

There are two types of garnishment, periodic (garnishes wages, for example, until the judgment is paid off) and non-periodic (garnishes a bank account or property). Even if a garnishment is ordered, the defendant has time to file objections.

Chapter 7

The Courthouse Wedding

The wedding was in my scheduling book for three weeks, a sign that the couple did some planning.

I called the bride and groom to the front of the courtroom. The bride said "We want the shortest ceremony you have." I looked at the groom, who nodded his approval.

"Short and sweet," he said. "The shorter the better."

This was very unusual, especially since this was the first marriage for each of them.

"There is one question I must ask you," I said. "If you answer correctly, I will sign the marriage license."

The lovebirds smiled longingly at each other.

"Do you come here freely and without reservation to give yourselves to each other in marriage?"

"I do," they said in unison.

"You are now husband and wife."

In less than two minutes from the time they walked into the courtroom, they were on their way out the door with a signed marriage license in their hands.

What A Bargain!

One of the biggest wedding-related bargains this side of Las Vegas is the courthouse wedding ceremony. For ten bucks, you get an official setting (or someplace outside of the courthouse, if the jurist is inclined to do so) and a jurist in a black robe asking you to repeat the magic words.

There are, however, a few things you should know if you are considering a courthouse wedding.

Civil Ceremony

When a jurist performs a wedding, it is a civil, as opposed to a religious, ceremony. There should be no references to the Almighty in a civil ceremony. (If it is done outside the courthouse and you work with the jurist beforehand, you may be able to work in some religious content. It depends on the jurist.)

The ceremony can take many forms and jurists sometimes work with the bride and groom to give them a ceremony they will like. I tried, when possible, to talk through the ceremony with the bride when she came to schedule the wedding. It helped things to go more smoothly for all of us on the big day.

Did I mention a bargain? The cost of a courthouse wedding is set by law at $10. It is against the law for a jurist to accept more money than that, even if he/she says they will donate it to charity.

If you feel that you must pay the jurist, donate that money to a charity. (Do not donate money in the jurist's name, since that has tax benefits for the jurist. Simply donate the money and mention it to the jurist, along with your thanks.) It removes any appearance of impropriety on the jurist's part. If the ceremony is held on a weekend outside the courthouse, you might invite the jurist and a guest to have dinner at the reception. I know of nothing prohibiting a jurist from accepting such an invitation.

Afterword

In his book, *Boss*, Mike Royko related how the late Chicago Mayor Richard J. Daley sat at his desk, patiently listening as unhappy citizens complained about one subject or another. After letting them vent, he asked them what he should do to fix the problem. If they had nothing to add, he lost his temper. Where were their programs and solutions, he demanded?

After reading that story many years ago, I realized that anyone can complain, but if the problem is big enough for you to complain about, you should take an equal amount of time to think about possible solutions. In this book, I offered some complaints about the court system. Let me now offer some possible solutions for consideration.

Court Reform

"Court Reform" is a term used by politicians, probably tested in focus groups, that sounds good in sound bites and brochures.

Real reform of the court system is possible and should be relatively easy to achieve, if everyone really wants it.

The first thing we need is a working group of about ten people, appointed by the Michigan Supreme Court, who are free of political affiliation and ambition, who cherish freedom, and are familiar with the legal system. SCAO staff should be available to help with questions and staff work as necessary.

If a serious request was made, I could supply the court with a list of names to choose from. It would, of course, ultimately be up to the court to decide what to do with the recommendations, but it is certainly worth considering.

Any reform must be well thought out. Court personnel must be allowed to comment freely and their suggestions must be seriously considered.

Okay, so it is not easy. It would, however, be worth the trouble.

One Court of Justice

One of the great frustrations in writing this book was the number of times I had to write a variation of "call the court." The state legislature and local governments, helped along by compliant judges, have in some ways made the courts into revenue collectors. The supreme court could reverse this so called "money grab."

According to the state's constitution, Michigan is supposed to have "one court of justice" with the supreme court sitting on top of the heap. Unfortunately, the administrative arm of the supreme court, the state court administrative office (SCAO), is treated by many of the state's judges as an impotent gnat. I do not exaggerate.

If the supreme court is going to set rules and standards, they should be adhered to. If judges do not follow rules, they should be sanctioned. The SCAO currently publishes for the courts a listing of fine and cost guidelines for civil infractions. Courts should be required to follow them. Trust me when I say that there will still be plenty of money left over at the end of the year. Which brings up another point.

Fines were supposed to go to libraries because it, presumably, took away the incentive for a police department to write tickets because they or their community needed more money. That incentive is gone.

I suggest that any fine money not going to libraries should be turned over to the state to fund the maintenance of Michigan's roads. Any costs not used by the court should go for the same purpose.

I have more suggestions, but that should do for starters.

About the Author

Russell B. Franzen spent a number of years in broadcasting before moving into the court system, where he served as a probation officer, magistrate, and court administrator. His free time is filled with historical research and writing. His previous book, *Squabble City*, is a story about political life in pioneer Michigan.

Appendix

Appendix 1

Traffic Accident?

One of the most misunderstood parts of the Michigan Vehicle Code involves traffic crashes (formerly called *accidents*).

A crash is normally caused by an act of negligence on the part of the driver. There are, however, true accidents. These are legally covered under what is called the "Sudden Emergency Doctrine."

If a situation occurs suddenly that you must react to and a crash results, you may not be responsible due to what is known as the "sudden emergency doctrine."

The Michigan appeals and supreme courts have made it clear over the years that to fall into this category, the situation must be different from the motorist's every day traffic routine ("unusual") or "take place so suddenly that the normal expectations of due and ordinary care" cannot be realized. [**Amick** v **Baller**, 102 Mich App 339, 341-341 (1980)]

Drivers normally use a "sudden emergency" as a defense in cases where they are charged with Failing to Stop in the Assured, Clear Distance

Ahead, also known as Driving Too Fast for Conditions or the Basic Speed Law.

Under the Basic Speed Law, MCL 257. 627(1), a driver, taking into account all factors around him/her, such as road and weather conditions, traffic volume, site limitations, must drive in a manner that allows the vehicle to stop within the distance between the front of his vehicle and whatever is ahead of it.

In Spillars v Simons, 42 Mich App 101, 105-106 (1972), the Court of Appeals ruled that the Sudden Emergency Doctrine does not include "every difficulty that a motorist encounters… The conditions must be extraordinary and totally unexpected."

Other cases applying to the Sudden Emergency Doctrine:

Walker v **Rebeuhr**, 255 Mich 204, 206 (1931); **Payton** v **Stealy**, 272 Mich 57, 62 (1935); **Socony Vacuum Oil Co.** v **Marvin** , 313 Mich 528, 546 (1946); **Vander Laan** v **Miedema,** 22 Mich App 170, 178 (1970); **Wright** v **Marzolf,** 34 Mich App 612 (1971); **Young** v **Flood**, 182 Mich App 538, 542-544 (1990); **Vsetula** v **Whitmyer**, 187 Mich App 675, 681-682 (1991); and **Hill** v **Wilson**, 209 Mich App 356, 358 (1995).

That is a lot of reading. If you think your traffic crash was a true accident, ask an attorney for advice.

Appendix 2

Thank You, Zolton!

In a landmark case [People v. Ferency, 133 Mich App 526 (1984)], Zolton Ferency was issued a speeding ticket by a police officer using a radar unit. He fought the case to the Michigan Court of Appeals.

In their ruling, the Court gave us what is known as the Ferency Doctrine. It basically says that in order to meet the 51% threshold, the following must be true:

—The radar unit must be certified by the Michigan Speed Measurement Task Force and properly installed in the police car,

—The officer must check the unit for accuracy before and after each shift, to ensure it is in proper working order,

—The officer must be a certified radar operator,

—The targeted vehicle must be within the operational beam of the radar and there must be nothing between the radar unit and the target vehicle to cause a false reading,

—There must be a tracking history on the target vehicle, which means the officer must make a visual observation, estimating the vehicle's speed as being above the posted speed limit, and that the visual observation, the doppler audio tone from the radar unit and the speed display must match.

— The speedometer on the police vehicle must be independently calibrated.

If all of the above are true, the 51% standard is met, and you lose your case. You can see that a radar or laser speeding ticket is hard to beat, but it can be done.

Appendix 3

Web Sites Of Interest

Many of the courts in Michigan have web sites that range from basic to wonderful. I will list those that I am aware of along with a few comments.

www.supremecourt.state.mi.us
This site has some great links to other courts in Michigan, as well as other legal sites. It is a very useful site.

www.circuit46.org
This is, in my opinion, the best of the Michigan court web sites. It is the site for 46th Circuit Trial Court in Crawford, Otsego, and Kalkaska counties. The trial court consists of the 46th Circuit Court, 83rd District Court, 87th District Court, and the Probate Courts for each of the three counties. In addition to good, basic information on the specific courts and the court system in general, it allows you to print off many of the court forms you might need.

www.ci.kalamazoo.mi.us/departments/court/l-index.htm
9th District Court, City of Kalamazoo

www.d12.com
12th District Court, Jackson County

ci.livonia.mi.us/services/16thdistrictcourt/courthome.htm
16th District Court, Livonia

www.24thdiscourt.org
24th District Court, Allen Park and Melvindale

www.voyager.net/34district
34th District Court, Romulus, Belleville, Huron Twp., Van Buren Twp., and Sumpter Twp.

www.co.kent.mi.us/courts.htm
Kent County Courts (*with links to the 63rd District and 17th Circuit Courts*)

www.ingham.org/dc/district.htm
55th District Court, Ingham County

www.co.washtenaw.mi.us/depts/courts/index.htm
Washtenaw County Trial Court (*with information on all courts in Washtenaw County, including 14A, 14B, and 15th District Courts*)

www.iserv.net/~dpasseng/grdc/grdcind.htm
61st District Court, City of Grand Rapids

www.co.ottawa.mi.us/dc/html
Ottawa County District Court

www.ingham.org/cc/circuit.htm
30th Circuit Court, Ingham County

www.midlandcounty.org/circuit
42nd Circuit Court, Midland County

www.midlandcounty.org/foc
42nd Circuit Court Friend of the Court, Midland County

www.libcoop.net/maccir
Macomb County Circuit Court

www.icle.org/michlaw/newcases.htm
This is the site of the Institute of Continuing Legal Education on which you can search for Supreme Court and Appeals Court decisions and court rules.

www.michiganlegislature.org/law
This is another search site, set up by the Michigan Legislature, that allows you to search the Michigan Compiled Laws, as well as new bills, legislative calendars, etc. A very good site.

www.pima.edu/dps/police.htm
This site has links to a lot of great law enforcement sites.

www.ingramcontent.com/pod-product-compliance
Lightning Source LLC
Chambersburg PA
CBHW021545200526
45163CB00015B/1646